Ethereum:

Strategies to Make Money with Ethereum

Gavin S. Finney

© **Copyright 2018 by Gavin S. Finney - All rights reserved.**

The contents of this book may not be reproduced, duplicated or transmitted without direct written permission from the author.

Under no circumstances will any legal responsibility or blame be held against the publisher for any reparation, damages, or monetary loss due to the information herein, either directly or indirectly.

Legal Notice:

This book is copyright protected. This is only for personal use. You cannot amend, distribute, sell, use, quote or paraphrase any part or the content within this book without the consent of the author.

Disclaimer Notice:

Please note the information contained within this document is for educational and entertainment purposes only. Every attempt has been made to provide accurate, up to date and reliable complete information. No warranties of any kind are expressed or implied. Readers acknowledge that the author is not engaging in the rendering of legal, financial, medical or professional advice. The content of this book has been derived from various sources. Please consult a licensed professional before attempting any techniques outlined in this book.

By reading this document, the reader agrees that under no circumstances are is the author responsible for any losses, direct or indirect, which are incurred as a result of the use of information contained within this document, including, but not limited to, —errors, omissions, or inaccuracies.

Table of Contents

Introduction

Chapter 1: Getting Started with Ethereum Strategies

Chapter 2: Setting Up a Strategic Plan

Chapter 3: Investing Strategy with Ethereum

Chapter 4: Trading with Ethereum

Chapter 5: Mining with Ethereum

Chapter 6: Crowdfunding Ethereum

Chapter 7: Buying and Holding Ethereum

Chapter 8: How to Have Safe Ethereum Exchanges

BONUS Chapter: Risk Management Strategies with Ethereum Investing

Conclusion

What This Book Will Teach You

Are you curious to learn about money making strategies from Ethereum but unsure where to start?

Have you always wanted to learn more about Ethereum and what strategies to implement, but are intimidated by the technical jargon being used?

If these questions relate well with you, then this book is for you. In this book, you will learn more about Ethereum and the strategies to make money in Ethereum.

Who this Book is for

This book contains information on how to learn

about Ethereum from a beginner level and focusing on Ethereum strategies.

Readers who can benefit the most from the book include:

- Individuals interested in making money from Ethereum
- Investing enthusiasts who want to learn about Ethereum as another possible source of income

    Readers who would like to know information about Ethereum

How this Book is Organized

This book is organized into three parts. The parts are best to be listened to in order. Once you become familiar with all the steps in the book, you can go directly to the techniques which apply to your current situation the best.

The three parts of the book are:

Part One outlines the strategic planning side on how to make money in Ethereum. The section also talks about the benefits of learning each topic in order to form a solid foundation in doing the right steps.

Part Two is about the Investing and Trading strategies in Ethereum and what investing mistakes you can avoid in order to help minimize the chances of you losing your money. You'll learn how the process works and how to implement the steps discussed.

Part Three are the other important topics on Ethereum such as:

- Risk Management
- Ethereum Mining

After each chapter, you will be provided with lessons and exercises in order to leverage the information found on this book.

By implementing the steps outlined on this book, you will be able to understand Ethereum strategies in helping you achieve your money-making goals.

Introduction:

Greetings reader! I would like to thank you for purchasing this book: *"Ethereum: Strategies to Make Money with Ethereum"* which is a continuation from the Beginner's Guidebook "Ethereum: Beginner's Simplified Guide to Make Money with Ethereum." The primary concept of this book is to take you through the different Ethereum strategies that can be implemented to earn money. This book will help you identify the game plan involved in making money by using Ethereum and the best way to choose the right strategy based on your money-making goals.

If you were a long-time cryptocurrency investor, you would have been quick enough to notice that 2017 turned out to be incredible for cryptocurrencies. This can be looked at as a starting point for digital currency revolution. The cryptocurrency market does turn a bit scary due to the fluctuation in its price value and fickleness of the virtual currency, but this doesn't stop the investors from investing in the coins. Being the first and most popular cryptocurrency in the market, Bitcoin is still considered as the initial choice when it comes to investing in crypto coins.

The high fees of Bitcoin and the slow transaction is at times not becoming suitable for payments as you end up spending the 'same fee' whether you buy a dinner or transfer $50,000. With many new cryptocurrencies coming into the market, the developers are making efforts to improvise on the blockchain technology, or rather use the technology to its full potential. Blockchains using 'smart contracts' technology are expected to have more opportunity in the future, and Ethereum is one such platform that uses this concept. These platforms can be used as an operating system to provide decentralized finance, banking, and commerce solutions. They can power a lot of applications.

It is important to have a strategic plan and select the right strategy to earn good money by using Ethereum. The chapters in the book will deal with the various Ethereum strategies that can be used and implemented based on your requirements. This year, 2018, looks promising for such technologies and it might even evolve and try to allow many new applications to use blockchain for secure transactions and storage.

By the time you finish the book, you will be able to understand the various Ethereum strategies and choose the ones that will best suit you. I hope this book serves as an informative and exciting read for you!

Happy reading!

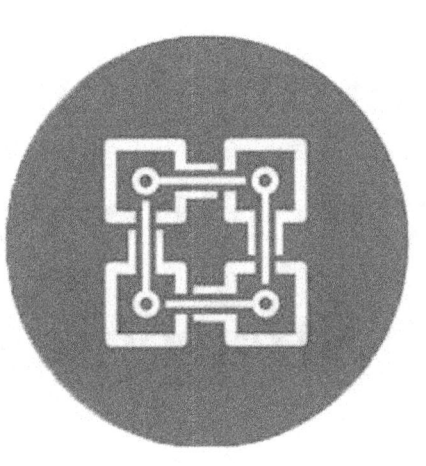

Chapter 1: Getting Started with Ethereum Strategies

ETHEREUM COIN

Chapter One: Getting Started with Ethereum Strategies

Before deciding to invest on Ethereum, it is essential to understand the complete 'know-how' of this new cryptocurrency and its underlying technology. With Bitcoin being the first official cryptocurrency to be introduced in the market in early 2009, it is crucial to understand why you should invest in Ethereum and what more it offers when compared to the first 'magic coin.' Bitcoins can be used only as cryptocurrency, but when it comes to Ethereum, this new platform offers numerous methods of exchange, smart contracts and the Ethereum Virtual Machine (EVM).

This platform offers an open source public service that uses blockchain technology to aid smart contracts and trade with cryptocurrencies in a secure manner without the involvement of a third party. Ethereum has two accounts available for the cryptocurrency users – the first one will be controlled by the private keys using manual intervention and the second one will be using 'smart contract' accounts (without manual intervention).

What is Ethereum Strategy?

It is essential to work out a formal plan when it comes to making money by using virtual currency apart from your usual 'hunches' and the 'luck factor.' Devising a strategy and implementing the same in the right way is necessary to avoid unnecessary monetary losses, which would have been the result of wrong decision-making. To attain the steady financial growth you expect, it is essential to follow a specific strategy pertaining to the cryptocurrency based on your objective of making money. Not taking the right decision, getting nervous at the time when decisions are to be taken, etc. can result in emotional outbreak thus pushing the investor to make a wrong choice.

Ethereum strategy will assist investors and traders to implement a well-calculated plan to make good returns with minimized losses. The goal of financial transactions shouldn't necessarily be 'making profits' or 'capitalizing on your returns.' It is crucial to understand that as an investor it is required to balance the 'prospective gains' to the 'risk of losses' to ensure the loss percentage is minimal.

Different Ethereum strategies can be followed to make some extra money, and we will be looking at a few of them in this book:

- Investing in Ethereum
- Trading with Ethereum
- Mining with Ethereum or Mining Ether
- Trying the long-term investment strategy – 'Buy and Hold.'
- Crowdfunding Ethereum

The most vital strategy would be to look at your current financial status and assess the amount of money that can be allocated to start your investment portfolio. If you already have an investment portfolio with traditional investing methods such as stocks, bonds, shares, etc., then it is important to segregate the percentage of the allocation you will have available to invest in Ethereum. It is advisable to purchase

Ether (ETH) between the range of 1% and 7% from your remaining allocation based on your risk tolerance level. It is better to 'start small' initially.

Historical basis behind the Ethereum Strategies

The founder of Ethereum – Vitalik Buterin, had already set the base for smart Ethereum strategies. Being an ardent supporter of Bitcoin, he had been working with blockchain technology since his early 20s, and the concept had impressed him so much that he came up with an improved feature which could allow users to use the blockchain technology for secure transactions specific to their own applications. The new platform – Ethereum was the start of a new cryptocurrency revolution as it allowed users or developers to use the platform as an operating system to code 'smart contracts' based on their requirements. Ether or ETH became the crypto token to 'fuel' the transactions that happened in the

Ethereum platform.

He then held on to his Ethers for a long time and then sold them for a good return at the right time. The founder of the coin himself implemented the long-term investment strategy by holding onto his coin for a specific period.

Importance of learning Ethereum Strategies

To be a successful Ethereum investor, it is essential to learn the various Ethereum Strategies that have been used and implemented in the cryptocurrency market. With uncertainty in the market trend and high price fluctuations, Ethereum investors need to be smart in devising a suitable strategic plan to ensure they get good returns.

Groundwork is essential – as an investor, you will need to understand the underlying technology the coin uses, the additional features it provides when compared to Bitcoin, the risk percentage involved in investing in Ether, etc. You will need to have complete knowledge of the Ethereum platform before you decide to invest your money on the same. Do your research well!

Minimum investment will be the right choice to start with. Don't rush, but take it slowly! Take some time before you invest more. Study the patterns, understand the trends and make the next move. Diversify your options – don't put all your money on one coin (Ether); invest in other crypto coins (if you are experienced) else try the traditional investment method (Stocks, bonds, etc.) along with your Ethereum investment. Example: Investing an equal amount of your investment allocation on Ether, Litecoin and Bitcoin will be a smart choice, as even if one coin's price value goes down drastically, you can make it up with the remaining crypto coins.

It is essential to understand the various Ethereum strategies and choose the ones that best suit your investment portfolio based on your needs. In doing so, you can reap benefits in the following ways:

- Will have clarity on the investment cycle
- Will be able to work towards a realistic profit expectation
- Can quickly decide on the right investment portfolio – be it long-term or short-term
- Will be able to understand the market much better and make analysis report concerning price fluctuations, comprehend the trade value breakdown, etc.
- Can easily study the various players in the market and work accordingly
- Will be able to determine the factor(s) which affects the change in price value
- Studying the suitable cryptocurrency exchanges and the options available for fund withdrawal

Strategizing your efforts allows you to gain better monetary rewards and helps you to become a successful investor with experience.

Overview to get the right Ethereum Strategy

An experienced investor or trader will fail if he or she doesn't have a good strategy to follow. So, it is of utmost importance to devise a proper strategic plan to help you earn the extra money you always wanted to make. The below-mentioned points need to be followed to help you with a good strategy:

- Select the right model by understanding the market pattern to make money by using Ethereum
- Choose the option which would best suit you – investment, trading, holding or crowdfunding
- Analyze your risk tolerance capability
- Decide and confirm your investment allocation, i.e. the amount of money you would want to 'put in.'
- Are you taking the money from your 'regular source of income' or do you have any other option?

- Plan a proper 'exit strategy' to ensure you don't get caught during the process
- Don't get overexcited and lose out on the capital. Follow the trend.
- It is crucial to be extra cautious and watchful when it comes to the 'trading options' as cryptocurrency trading is open 'round the clock.'
- Don't repeat your earlier mistakes. Make a record and revisit them if necessary
- Buy low and sell high
- Don't get into mining unless you are ready to invest a good amount for the initial mining setup, but if you are confident and have experience in Ethereum mining, it is advisable to continue as it a good long-term investment plan.
- Crowdfunding Ethereum is a good option if you are looking at starting your own project or planning to donate to a charity

CHAPTER SUMMARY:

The chapter will help you get a brief picture of the following:

- Ethereum strategy
- Importance of Ethereum strategy
- Benefits of devising a strategy
- Overview of steps to be followed for implementing the best strategy

YOUR QUICK START ACTION STEP:

You will have got a basic idea of what Ethereum strategy is, the necessity to use the same and the benefits one gets while implementing the strategy. The next step will be to learn quite a bit more about the various ways to make money by using Ethereum, but before that, it is essential to have in-depth knowledge of the said cryptocurrency. You can learn more about Ethereum by visiting the site: https://coincentral.com

Chapter 2: Setting Up a Strategic Plan

Chapter Two: Setting Up a Strategic Plan

It is difficult to achieve anything without a proper plan – be it the traditional investment or cryptocurrency investment. To make it simple, even to arrange a small family party, you will need to plan things to ensure there are no hitches in the arrangements.

What is a Strategic Plan? Analyzing all the things that are necessary for your 'small investment' to work and then narrowing it down to the things that are 'actually needed' for it to work better to acquire a unique and positive result can be referred to as 'strategic planning'.

By the time you are done with the analysis process, your rough plan looks extensive and exhaustive. It is now time to scrutinize the process even more and finalize on the accurate method to get the expected outcome. You might feel that developing a proper strategic plan is such a meticulous process, but when you break it down it is easy to attempt.

It is vital to have a proper strategic plan when it comes to cryptocurrency as, unlike the traditional stock market exchanges, the volatility and the risk involved in the crypto market are incredibly high.

Strategic planning for Ethereum

Defined strategy, suitable decision, proper allocation, etc. will be the outcome of proper planning. Trying this five-step approach will help in developing a suitable strategic plan to help finalize on the right Ethereum strategies to be implemented:

- Have a definite picture of your financial outcome
- Focus on the necessities
- Define the objectives
- Set the accountability
- Assess and review

When you identify the steps as mentioned earlier with respect to Ethereum, you will be able to come up with an appropriate strategic plan for which you will have to check the following:

- What is your picture of the financial outcome when it comes to Ethereum? Are you interested in cashing out regularly or are you planning for long-term returns?
- What is your requirement when it comes to making money? Why do you want to look at Ethereum as your option? Are you expecting 'big money' as returns?
- Do you have an objective for your financial investment? Are you looking at long-term retirement plans or are you looking at making some extra money to stabilize your financial portfolio?
- You are accountable for the money you invest so it is crucial to decide on the total amount of money you want to 'put in' on Ethereum investment. How much can you afford to lose?
- Decide on the total time period you are planning to wait for the investment to mature, select the right cryptocurrency

exchange, choose a secure coin wallet to store your ether, etc.

- Before you get into action, assess your plan again and review it. Check if you want to make any changes in the same before you finalize it.

Example of Ethereum failure

If you don't know the cryptocurrency well, it is better not to jump into it without understanding the market and devising a proper strategic plan. We shall tell you about an Ethereum investor who lost the majority of his capital investment, as he didn't know the currency too well.

Two years ago, there was a post on Reddit in which a trader posted about how he made a wrong decision and lost all his ether. This person had read about Ethereum and was tempted by the returns it could provide considering the increased price value the coin had then. Without making any attempt to understand the coin and devising a strategy, he went ahead with his idea by investing all his life savings on Ether. He bought around 4000 ETH at 0.003500 price and instead of holding on to them, he started panic-selling the coins whenever there was a price decrease or whenever he felt the market was going to crash down.

On top of this, he had also been buying more Ether when he felt that the price would spike high after which it wouldn't be possible for him to catch the coin later. He continued doing this for quite some time unless he had only 500 ETH left and ended up melting his money (the majority of the capital amount).

If he had worked out a proper plan and set out his objectives clearly as in – what was his estimated profit expectation? How much would he want to invest? Was he looking at a long-term benefit or short-term benefit? Etc., he wouldn't have lost it all. Those 4000 ETH would have made 'big money' if he had just held the coins.

Inference:

- Don't try to be smarter than the market if you don't know how to play with the coins. Just buy and hold!
- Don't take decisions when you are emotional (fear – in his case). Panic selling is the biggest mistake an investor can make!
- Don't buy when the price is high. Follow *buy low and sell high* idea!
- Don't ever invest with your 'lifesavings,' i.e., the only savings you have or the amount you can afford to lose.

Importance of Strategic planning

If you want to be a smart Ethereum investor, it is essential to be clear about your objectives and plan things ahead – be they big or small. Drafting a strategic plan will make sure you don't get caught in between the investment or trading process and enjoy good returns. When you know what you are doing and why you are doing it, then automatically the outcome will also be as expected.

The important points one can notice when you have a proper strategic plan in place are:

- You will be able to serve the purpose of your goals as you have a clear-cut picture of the financial outcome you expect
- There will be more clarity in the ideas you get, which ultimately helps to focus on the right upshot.
- Since you have your objectives defined clearly, you (as an investor or trader) will be able to make good use of your time, energy and investment.
- As you hold the accountability of your chosen strategy, you double-check on the investment made and review the process at regular intervals
- Revisiting the previous mistakes and assessing the process again to ensure earlier mistakes aren't repeated will prevent unnecessary monetary losses.

When you know your goals and work towards the same with a planned approach, the strategy you choose will automatically give the required results you have been expecting.

Having a thorough understanding of Ethereum, going through the technology it uses and keeping yourself updated on the 'smart contracts' technology can help you earn good money. If you have prepared a proper strategic plan for making money by using Ethereum, you will be getting the following benefits:

- You will be able to choose the right mode of investment platform or trading platform as you have already set the framework clear.
- Helps to concentrate on making profits as your direction is already set on the right path
- Easy to decide on the expected benefits – long term or short term!
- Since you already have a plan in place, it is easy to manage the risks that arise due to market fluctuations.
- Helps you decide with 'clear head' without allowing emotions to control you

Steps to come up with a Strategic Plan

If you are new to the world of cryptocurrency, then you definitely need to come up with a plan before you plunge onto the bandwagon. Let us look at the general steps that will help you devise a good strategic plan for Ethereum:

- Start by doing a substantial amount of research on Ethereum – the platform and Ether - the crypto coin.
- Study the market table of Ethereum and its ICO periods (Initial Coin Offering)
- Do your own due diligence and get into intense research activity. Don't get greedy!
- Don't go rushing to buy the coins whenever you see an increase in the price value. Always buy when the price is low, but before buying ask yourself – Is it the right time now?
- If you are planning to do day trading, you are at a riskier spot in the market. Even experienced trader's fail!

- Study the white paper clearly and understand the nuances of Ether

CHAPTER SUMMARY:

This chapter will help you get familiar with the following:

- Strategic planning for Ethereum.
- Importance of Strategic planning
- Example of Ethereum failure due to lack of planning
- Steps to help devise a good strategic plan

YOUR QUICK START ACTION STEP:

It is important to have an in-depth understanding of Ethereum as a platform and Ether as a currency to ensure you devise a proper strategic plan. You can visit https://blog.ethereum.org to learn more about Ethereum. To be good in designing the right strategy, you will need to understand the various development programs they offer and keep yourself updated. You can browse through the site: https://blog.ethereum.org/2018/01/02/ethereum-scalability-research-development-subsidy-programs/

Chapter 3: Investing Strategy with Ethereum

Chapter Three: Investing Strategy with Ethereum

If you are a beginner in Ethereum, it is critical to deal with your anxiety when the 'price swings' happen more often than not. This will require a lot of discipline, especially when the cryptocurrency market is known for its extreme volatility. All this excitement of 'gaining more return than your capital investment', 'making massive profit', etc. can get contagious, but it is essential to get the basics right before deciding to expand your investment portfolio with a coin which is entirely new to you.

Ether (ETH), the crypto token of Ethereum platform, has lately gone up to $1,000 per ETH with the market cap of Ether touching $98 billion which makes it hold the third place among the most valuable 'blockchain' list.

Ethereum Investing Strategy

When you decide to invest in the crypto token 'Ether,' you are taking a premeditated decision that has its own set of rewards along with risks. Before you go ahead with your Ethereum Investment decision, you ought to have asked the following questions:

- Why should I invest in Ether?
- Will investing in this crypto coin give me more profits?
- Does it have an easy fund withdrawal option?
- Should I put in any special effort in to store the Ether securely?
- Do I have a 'right time' to invest in Ether?
- How do I decide when to sell my Ether?
- Is there any particular strategy that I should follow?

Ethereum Investment Strategy helps the investor to analyze and assess his current financial status, the need to invest in the coin and the possible monetary outcome he is looking at. It is crucial to set the goals clearly, define the objectives and devise the right plan and work towards the direction of the plan. The investment strategy helps you get the basics right-

- Understand your financial expectation from Ethereum investment
- Decide the maximum amount of money you can 'put in' to this cryptocurrency
- Getting the facts right about – Investing only 'that amount' of money which you can afford to lose in case the result doesn't come out as expect
- Determining the best possible investment approach that will work for you based on your current financial status, risk, and real-time profit expectation
- Making up your mind on the benefits of long-term or short-term investment and taking a decision on choosing either of them or both
- Playing safe by 'holding' or taking a risk by 'short-term trading'.

Your investment strategy becomes clear and transparent when you know what you want as mentioned above which automatically helps you get the desired financial result.

Are you sure about your Ethereum Strategy?

As an investor, you need to be sure about where you are investing your funds and the flexibility the portfolio provides when you need to access those funds. Patience is the key to a smart investor, as he understands that investment is not a swift venture, but a 'not-so-slow process' either, which will need you to hold back and watch for the funds to scale. If you are looking to achieve your investment objective, you need to focus on the 'trends'.

Your investment strategy on Ethereum should consider the following points to ensure you don't get 'tangled' in the mess of 'cryptocurrency investment graph:'

Be careful with 'unnecessary chattering.'

Don't take decisions based on discussions which don't have a 'valid justification' when it comes to cryptocurrency. When Ethereum first came onto the market, there was a unanimous uproar mentioning that this platform will stumble down very soon as it offered a 'customized blockchain' option, which was not available in Bitcoin. Ether was referred as 'shitcoin' as the developers kept improvising the code. When you are strong with the basics (Ethereum as a platform and the features it offers), you will be smart enough to differentiate between the 'talks' and 'facts.'

Keep yourself updated by following the news on Ethereum on Twitter – if you are an Ethereum investor, the following are a few of the best people to follow to know the 'facts:'

- Brian Armstrong (Coinbase Founder)
- Laura Shin (Crypto Senior Editor - Forbes)
- Vlad Zamfir (Ethereum developer – currently working on 'Casper Proof of stake' protocol)
- Vitalik Buterin (Ethereum co-founder)

Invest only if you know it well

It is vital to know the fundamental value of Ethereum to help you take the right decision when it comes to 'selling the coin.' If you have filled yourself with half-baked information, then you end up taking the worst decisions when it comes to Ether. A similar situation happened when China officially announced that it was banning ICOs, which caused 'panic' among most of the Ethereum investors because they didn't understand the cryptocurrency clearly.

If you were someone who knew Ethereum well, then you would also know that ICOs was a popular use-case and the actual importance of the Ethereum blockchain expands to restructuring the social, political and economic systems. Do extensive researches before you invest!

Protect your Ether

When you are investing in a portfolio (cryptocurrency), which is known for its high volatility, it becomes your responsibility to secure your Ether carefully. Storing your coins in online exchanges is not recommended, as you never know when the exchange will get hacked or exploited. To avoid such platform risks, choose the best hardware wallet and store it.

Check the 'Cost Averaging'

Most of the popular cryptocurrencies, such as Bitcoin, Litecoin and Ethereum have gone through unmatched regularity breaking the 'all-time highs.' Many investors panic when the price value goes high, and they have 'less coins' held – they think if it is going high, I had better buy the coin right away. This is wrong! Either purchase at regular intervals when the price goes low or keep a check on the 'cost average' and determine the price averaged over the time to make your next move.

Cost average means buying Ether for a specific number of weeks or months at regular intervals irrespective of the price value to determine the 'price average'.

Balance your portfolio

It is always better to 'buy and hold' your Ether rather than going for 'day trading' to minimize the losses in your portfolio. You can also balance your investment portfolio by having a diversified approach – try investing in Bitcoin, ether, Litecoin, etc. by defining the percentage spread based on your investment allocation, i.e., if the market cap of the coin is less, then let the investment percentage be the lowest.

Acquire Profit

Once you have done all the above-mentioned steps, it is now time to 'take profits.' Go for a long-term investment strategy to get good returns as most serious Ethereum investors will vote for the 'Buy and Hold' strategy, as this will give significant gains on your Ether. When you take a percentage of your 'returns' as profit that is when you have succeeded as an investor.

Investment Strategies (Examples)

One might want to invest in Ether or buy the coin for various reasons.

- Buying Ethereum for Use (to pay wages globally, to use EVMs and

smart contracts, to interact with blockchain based IoT (Internet of Things) devices)
- Buying Ethereum as an Investment (to diversify a conventional portfolio, hedge against incumbent fiat system, access other blockchain investments or token sales)

Each investment strategy is different, and their suitability is subject to one's own risk tolerance to the respective financial portfolio. Let us look at the two frequently used Ethereum investment strategies:

Buy and Hold

Buying the coin 'Ether' and holding them for a considerably longer period will prove to be extensively beneficial to most Ethereum investors due to the following possibilities:

- If it ever replaces fiat currencies, the value will be 'unbelievably high.'
- If it becomes the 'digital currency of choice' for all web-related payments, it

would allow billions of devices to handle efficient transactions internationally.

An experienced Ethereum investor might consider DCA (dollar cost averaging) as an option when he is looking to buy Ether given the 'current volatility of the cryptocurrency'.

Buy and Diversify

If you say you can predict the future of Ethereum, you will become a 'laughing stock' among cryptocurrency investors. Though it is true that Ethereum has shown its predecessor 'Bitcoin' that - the once little-known crypto asset can become a dominant force in a small period, it is always better to be cautious with the investment made on any new crypto coin. Example: If you are an experienced cryptocurrency investor and have been trading using various crypto coins, then it is always a wise idea to purchase Ether in exchange for the other new crypto coins – be it Ripple or Monero or Bytecoin to avoid losses which can occur due to unforeseen losses of either of the new coins. Though there is a possibility of anyone's coin to crumple down completely, many technologists (especially the ones working on distributed systems) are claiming that crypto assets will become omnipresent in the future.

Benefits of Ethereum Investing Strategies

If you are looking at becoming a successful Ethereum investor, it is essential to have an in-depth functional knowledge of the platform and the crypto token to help in devising a suitable strategic plan that adheres to your requirements. Being aware of your investment goal, understanding the necessity of investment, allocating an amount best suited to your financial status and creating a work plan to manage the investment portfolio as this will help you in making the right strategy.

When you know your Ethereum investing strategies, then you are benefitted by the following:

- You will be able to see the outcome as expected
- Working out early on the risk management strategies
- You will get into 'review' mode once in a month or every quarter to check if there is a necessity to change the strategy.
- You will also be giving a thought about deciding the necessity to keep purchasing Ether at regular intervals to gain better profits.
- Checking out the average price value fluctuation
- Diversifying the investment portfolio to get better gains and reduce the risk of losing out on the capital amount.

Investing Strategy – Let us try!

We shall try the 'buy and hold' strategy to help you have a safe Ethereum investment if you are a beginner. Based on the exchange you choose, the process of purchasing Ether will differ, but when you look at it, in general, all of them have the same principles. Let us get started by following the below- mentioned steps:

- Get registered in a suitable cryptocurrency exchange (do your own research and finalize on the best one which suits you. Coinbase, eToro or LocalEthereum are considered to be good)
- During the process of registration, most of the exchanges do 'identity checks', KYC (Know Your Customer) and AML (Anti-Money Laundering) checks.
- Once you have your account verified, you will have to photo identification and proof of address to continue further.
- You can now choose your 'deposit method' – each exchange offers their own banking methods, which can be PayPal, wire transfers, card payments or SEPA. There will be a fee charged for each deposit method, so you can choose the one that suits your needs.
- After choosing the deposit method, you will have to deposit fiat currencies based

on your location. The time to get the money deposited from your traditional bank to your exchange account may vary from 24 hours to 72 hours based on the method and exchange you choose.

- Once the amount has been credited to your exchange account, you can use the fiat money to purchase your Ether. (To make this process easier, choose the exchanges which are beginner-friendly. eToro, Coinbase, Plus500, Bitpanda, LocalEthereum, Bitstamp, GDAX, Gemini, and Kraken are popularly used exchanges out of which Bitstamp, Bitpanda, Plus500, Coinbase, and eToro are beginner-friendly)
- After you have initiated the 'buy request' for the Ether based on your investment amount, you will get the coins credited to your online wallet in the exchange once the seller has received the money
- The Ether, which is now available in your online wallet, will need to be transferred to an offline wallet or

hardware wallet for storing the coin safely.
- You can now hold on to your Ether for a specific period (preferably six months to 1 year to start with) and then trade the coin once the period matures.

CHAPTER SUMMARY:

This chapter will have helped you get a clear understanding of the following:

- Ethereum Investing Strategy
- Importance of understanding the investment strategy
- Things to remember before you choose your strategy
- Example of Ethereum Investment strategy
- Benefits of following the strategy

YOUR QUICK START ACTION STEP:

Now that you have understood the basics of Ethereum Investment Strategy, it is time for you to get into action. Read through the blogs, forums and 'how-to' guides that are dedicated to Ethereum investments. If you would like to be more cautious in choosing your strategy, it is advisable to update yourself on anything and everything about Ethereum. You can visit the site: https://ethereumprice.org to know more about the price value and the trade history.

Chapter 4: Trading with Ethereum

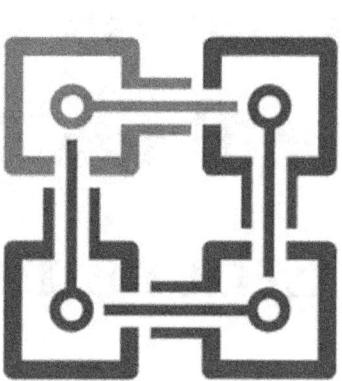

Chapter Four: Trading with Ethereum

In 2014, Ethereum was introduced to the market as the first blockchain which offers robust 'Smart Contract' technology, i.e., it provided a 'customized blockchain' enabling the developers and users to create a tailor-made blockchain app suiting their respective requirements. It also became the first platform to have an ICO use-case by crowdfunding numerous cryptocurrency projects via ICO (Initial Coin Offerings) in the Ethereum platform. Ethereum allows users to purchase blockchain-secured virtual real estate hosts Decentraland, a Virtual Reality Environment.

The crypto token 'Ether' which is used to 'fuel' the Ethereum platform has already been recognized as a popular cryptocurrency since the time its price value showed good hike with a solid market cap. Ethereum offers a 'steadier base' to trade when compared to Bitcoin. Trading, in general, is a risky business due to the market volatility and when it comes to cryptocurrency, it becomes even more complicated as the 'fluctuation is way too high' when compared to the traditional stock market exchange.

Ethereum Trading Strategy

Ethereum Trading requires a lot of patience and discipline, as there is no assurance that you will attain constant profit in returns. It is essential to trade Ether with reliable and trusted cryptocurrency exchange traders, who are otherwise referred to as 'trading brokers'. Many of these trading brokers offer multiple Ether pairs, such as ETH/USD (Ether/USD), ETH/BTC (Ether/Bitcoin), etc.

It is advisable to trade Ether at 'zero leverage' due to the volatility of ether, but the considerable growth, which is seen in the price value of Ether makes 'buy and hold' as an excellent strategy to be followed. When it comes to trading, it is essential to analyze the previous trading patterns and the price value fluctuations to predict the market of the coin to a certain extent.

The price value of Ether is affected mostly by either of the following reasons:

- The ongoing development of the Ethereum platform does affect the price value of its crypto token, as it is still not a matured currency.
- The expansion in Ethereum blockchain and its related Dapps also affects the price value as 'Ether' is originally the crypto token used to pay for the computational services and the transactions that happen in the Ethereum platform.
- Another major factor that affects the price value of this coin is the 'price of its predecessor – Bitcoin'. Whenever Bitcoin experiences an increase in price value, Ether does see a change in its value table consecutively.

Ethereum Trading Strategy is the process that helps the trader to check on the 'capital maintenance,' analyze the trade size, devise an exit strategy, and understand the liquidity flow. When a proper trading strategy is devised based on his capital amount or the already held crypto coins, it becomes less difficult for the trader to choose the Ethereum strategy that best suits his requirement.

It is crucial to check your current financial strength, analyze the risk tolerance capacity, evaluate the trade size, formulate a proper exit plan and keep track of the data feeds in the Ethereum market when you decide on the trading strategy.

Examples of Ether Trading Strategies

When it comes to this crypto coin 'Ether,' there are two basic trading strategies that are usually implemented:

- Buy and Hold
- Active Trading

Buy and Hold

Most of the traders believe that there is definitely a growing potential in all the popular cryptocurrencies, especially, Ether, which is why many are following the 'Buy and Hold' strategy. Purchasing Ether and putting it in cold storage (buying a coin and securing them without performing any transactional activity) is the best way to make long-term benefits. You can use paper wallets or hardware wallets to store your coins securely.

The best 'buy and hold' solution would most likely be a combination of a hardware wallet and paper wallet.

Active Trading

This strategy allows the traders to take advantage of short-term moves with a focus on high liquidity flows. It is considered to be the most speculative trading. When it comes to cryptocurrency, active trading is a bit tough as not all exchanges offer this option. To perform active trading, the trader will have to set 'pending orders' and 'stop-limit/stop losses'.

In such cases, you will have to set alerts in the exchange you use so that you keep track of the market movements and manually place trades. Coinbase doesn't allow 'pending orders' so active trading will need to be done manually using another trade broker app.

One of the most irritating problems active traders face with exchanges is the complexity in storing fiat currency. This can be considered as a potential risk with Ether trading as every time you want to convert Ether to fiat money, you will have to go through multiple hoops, i.e., when you sell the Ether, you will have to transfer the money to your bank account and then send it back to your exchange to buy another coin again. *Issue*: You might have to wait for a week every time you transfer money to and from the bank account.

Is it beneficial to follow an Ethereum Trading Strategy?

Even an experienced trader will fail if he or she does 'blindfold trading' without a proper trading plan. It is therefore essential to choose the best Ethereum strategy and implement the same to get some good profits. Let us try to understand this with an example – in case you are an experienced cryptocurrency trader who has been using multiple crypto coins, you will need to have a clear flow of your investment and trading strategies to ensure you don't lose money. Let's say you have been accumulating Ether by trading the altcoins you had held on to; then you will first need to analyze the market cap of the 'altcoins you were holding' and its total value when compared to Ether's market cap. Next, you will have to decide how often you will be trading the altcoins for Ether and determine the 'time period' accordingly. When you have your plan clear, you get to grow your ETH stack and, with time, it keeps growing automatically.

The benefits of choosing the right strategy will help you in:

- Predicting the trading volume approximately

- Ability to analyze the previous trading history and have a realistic 'return estimation.'
- Understanding the liquidity flow and market fluctuation to decide on the next move
- Being extra cautious before you finalize on your trading option

Ethereum Trading Strategy – Let us try!

We will be looking at the steps needed to be taken to implement the 'Buy and Hold' trading strategy:

- Creating an account in a trusted cryptocurrency exchange services which allow you to directly buy Ether (few exchanges will require you to buy a Bitcoin first and then exchange it for your desired coin)
- Changelly and ShapeShift are the two exchanges which don't need you to sign up for trading

- Once you have created the account, verified and confirmed the same; you will have to fund your exchange account with fiat money so that you can purchase your 'Ether.'
- Transfer the 'Ether' coins to your hardware wallet from the online wallet in exchange
- Secure the coins with two-factor authentication (if needed).
- Hold on to the coins for a specific period and depending on the price value increase at that particular time, trade the coin for 'fiat money' to get some profits or trade it for another crypto coin to 'capitalize on your return'.

CHAPTER SUMMARY:

This chapter gives you a brief picture of the following:

- Ethereum Trading
- Different Ethereum Trading Strategies

- Importance of understanding the strategies
- Benefits of using the Ethereum Trading strategies
- Examples of Ethereum Trading Strategies

YOUR QUICK START ACTION STEP:

Now that you have understood the basic trading strategies that need to be followed while trading with Ether, it is time for you to implement the one that best suits you. You can keep yourself updated on all the Ethereum based investment and trading news by visiting the site: https://blog.ethereum.org/

Chapter 5: Mining with Ethereum

Chapter Five: Mining with Ethereum

Mining is considered to be one of the long-term investment strategies, which is implemented by most cryptocurrency investors. Apart from purchasing Ether through cryptocurrency exchanges, one can acquire the crypto token by following the 'Ethereum mining' process. Similar to Bitcoin mining, it is possible to mine 'Ether' and generate profits. The miner is rewarded with 5 Ether (ETH) every time a new block is verified and looking at the current price value, five tokens of Ether will approximately come up to $10,000. Unlike Bitcoin network where a block data is verified every ten minutes, the Ethereum network allows the miners to verify the block data every twenty seconds, thus increasing the transactional speed, generating more crypto tokens with comparatively less mining difficulty.

It is possible to mine Ether using CPU or GPU mining, but the former is not cost-effective when compared to the latter. To set up a mining lab, one will need a good computer, high-computing processor, graphics card with 2 GB RAM (minimum) and mining software. If you want to do CPU mining, you will need to ensure you have a lot of memory space on your hard drive with excellent computation power.

The miner will verify the block of transactions that are pending using the 'proof of work' concept to solve the 'hash' – EtHash. The miners are offered 5 ETH and paid a verification fee for every 'successful' verification of the transaction block. Similar to Bitcoin mining, mining Ether requires a lot of electricity and massive computational power. The Ethereum blockchain can also be used to create 'Smart contracts' which works like digital contracts where you can update the required conditions for the contract to work and if the set conditions are satisfied, the smart contracts can be executed when it gets automatically triggered without any external verification

Ethereum Mining Strategy

The decentralized way of maintaining the existing transaction and verifying new transaction by solving complex cryptographic puzzle using the concept of 'Proof of Work' makes the process of mining strictly secure and intact. The absolute consensus among the participating nodes in the Ethereum network ensures there is no possible fraudulent activity. The solution time, which is 20 seconds, can be averaged to 12-15 seconds approximately.

The developer team of Ethereum platform is working on another algorithm 'Proof of stake' which might very soon avoid the necessity of miners to mine the crypto token. In this new concept, the developers are working on the 'Proof of stake' algorithm where the Ethereum network is secured directly by the owner of the crypto tokens 'Ether.' This new algorithm will help in achieving 'distributed consensus' using fewer resources compared to the 'absolute consensus' theory in the current 'Proof of Work' concept.

The Ethereum Mining Strategy is the process that allows the investor to decide on the best possible mining plan based on his capital investment and the expected profit gain. The three most commonly used mining strategies are:

CPU Mining

Ether can be mined using CPU mining if you have a good computer, high-end processor, CPU with good memory storage, the Ethereum Mining pools and the mining software. Though one can mine Ether with CPU at any place provided the above-mentioned hardware setup is available, the result might not be cost-effective, as the process requires a lot of electricity and computational power. With only CPU as the major mining rig, the process might be slow and frustrating which might result in lesser profit.

GPU Mining

The ASIC mining hardware might not be suitable for Ethereum since the introduction of 'proof of stake' concept that restricts the mining process to 'GPU Mining'. This automatically reduces the investment cost the miners will have to spend on the hardware, thereby favoring home regulars when compared to the big-time investors. In this strategy, the investor (i.e., miner) will need the following Ethereum mining rig:

- Graphics card
- Storage (HDD or secondary)
- RAM
- Motherboard
- Ethernet
- Power Supply Unit

Getting a good graphics card will determine how profitable your Ethereum mining rig will be.

Ethereum Cloud Mining

Cloud Mining Services don't require the investor to spend on logistics as the cloud service provider will help with the already existing mining facilities based on the user's expectation on the 'amount of hash power' he will need to mine his crypto token. This hash power is the mining power that the service uses to mine the Ether for you. There are different types of cloud mining services, such as Leased hashing power, Virtual hosted mining and Hosted mining.

The cloud mining service providers help by leasing the 'hash power' to their clients in *'Leased hashing power'* service. *Virtual hosted mining* service leases the processing power and memory to the client, which can be used for their mining purposes. In *hosted mining* service, the clients are provided with leased machines to help in their mining process. It is wise to double-check the authenticity and reliability of the cloud mining services as there have been proven reports of scammers in this area.

Importance of Ethereum Mining Strategies

It is important to choose the right strategy to mine the Ether for the following reasons:

- Ethereum Mining productivity
- Mining algorithm used in Ethereum

Ethereum Mining Productivity refers to the productivity the miners receive while using the respective mining strategy to mine the Ether. This productivity is based on two main factors – Electricity and hardware (the mining rig). The returns you get in mining can differ crazily as whenever the price value decreases, the revenue related to the electricity and hardware costs will also reduce. Cryptocurrency's volatile nature does affect the mining process to any extent, but if you are smart enough to choose good hardware and the right energy source, you can definitely make a substantial amount of income.

If you would like to conclude on your 'profit projection' you can use the online Ethereum mining profitability calculation tools to check your estimated returns. Remember, your mining profit is directly linked to your energy and hardware investment.

The mining algorithm used in Ethereum has

been a point of discussion since 2016 due to the new algorithm 'Proof of Stake' which is trying to replace the 'Proof of Work' algorithm completely. This new algorithm is referred to as Casper Proof of Stake, and it has a good number of advantages over the Bitcoin's 'Proof of Work' algorithm:

- It requires less computational power
- It is more reliable as this new algorithm concentrates on speed and availability over regularity which results in faster validations
- Proof of Work uses hardware to generate the computation value while Proof of Stake looks at miner-less approach that reduces the network of huge energy requirements.

Choosing the right mining strategy can definitely benefit the investor in various ways such as:

- Possibility of mining more coins
- Increase in profitability

- Less complication in setting up the hardware requirements
- Right choice of Ethereum mining pool can result in 'less complex algorithm' to be solved

Though there are many ways to mine Ether, choosing the best way that suits your needs will determine your profit expectation. Hardware mining or cloud mining – whichever option is chosen, it is vital to research the process, concepts and the hardware involved in the same. The amount you invest in hardware and energy (electricity) will give you an approximate estimation of your returns.

Mining Strategy – Let us try!

Let us look at how to get started with mining using GPU mining strategy. If you are a beginner in Ethereum mining, you should be able to get started if you have a good computer with a Windows operating system and a powerful GPU card. The below-mentioned steps can help you get started with the process:

- *Install the video card drivers* by first downloading the GPU drivers from amd.com. Select the 'Support & Drivers' option on the site, type the GPU details (the type of product, product family, product name and operating system) and click 'Display Results'.
- The search result display window will show the GPU driver you have chosen. You can download the driver by clicking on the 'Download' button next to the driver details else you can choose the 'Download Previous Drivers and Software' to choose the older versions (which are said to be excellent drivers for mining based on your graphics card).
- If you want to work with NVIDIA drivers, then you can log in to https://www.geforce.com/drivers to get the latest ones.
- *Install the GPU drivers* and reboot the system. Go to the Device Manager and check if the GPU has been installed properly (Note: Ensure you don't have

any warning signs. If you do, uninstall and reinstall)
- After your GPU card is ready, *get the Ethereum Wallet Address* by installing an Ethereum wallet from MyEtherWallet.com
- Have a strong password for your wallet and click 'Create New Wallet', then download the Keystore file and click 'I understand. Continue' button
- The next window will show the 'Private Key,' save the same
- You will need to unlock the wallet to see your wallet address. Click the 'Save Your Address' button and then choose the 'Keystore File' radio button and click 'Select Wallet File.'
- Browse to the location where you have stored the recently downloaded 'Keystore File' (starts with UTC...) and select the same.
- Enter the password (as you will be prompted to do so) and click the 'Unlock your wallet' button.

- Scroll down to view your wallet address in the 'Your Address' label. Save the same as this is the Ethereum wallet address which will be used for mining
- It is now time to download the Claymore Ethereum Miner from https://Bitcointalk.org/index.php?topic=1433925.0
- Extract the file to your desktop once downloaded
- You will need to *change a few Windows Settings before mining,*
    - Go to Power Settings and set it to 'Never turn off/sleep.'
    - Modify the system page file and manually set it to 16384 MB
    - If you are looking at having an undisturbed mining process, you can turn off the Windows Updates, but if you feel it is more secure to leave it ON, you will need to understand that your system might restart during

automatic updates disrupting the mining process.
- o Add an exception to your anti-virus program or Windows Defender by including 'EthDcrMiner64.exe' as a trustable file so that the software doesn't flag it as a threat and disable the file
- *Choose the right Ethereum mining pool* (preferably Nanopool or Etheremine) and configure the mining bat file. Note: You can Google the steps based on the mining pool you select
- Once your mining pool is ready, double click the bat file to start the miner.

CHAPTER SUMMARY:

This chapter would have helped you understand the following:

- Ethereum mining strategy
- Importance of Ethereum mining strategies

- Example of GPU mining strategy

YOUR QUICK START ACTION STEP:

Now that you have understood the basics of mining and have clarity on the different Ethereum mining strategies, you can get started with GPU mining by following the steps mentioned in the earlier section.

Chapter 6: Crowdfunding Ethereum

Chapter Six: Crowdfunding Ethereum

There are regulations, which need to be followed when it comes to crowdfunding, such as, the eligibility criteria of people who are interested in investing and the maximum amount they can invest. These regulations are necessary to prevent investors from going bankrupt, as there are possibilities of 'not-so-wealthy' investors investing their savings to a crowdfunding project that is actually too risky for the investor. Not all startups or projects started via crowdfunding get to succeed and to avoid the investors facing the risk of losing their 'capital amount' if the said project fails, crowdfunding concepts are regularized.

Crowdfunding – in general

Crowdfunding is the process by which new projects can be financed, or charity money can be raised, or an art exhibition can be set up when several investors come together by putting in small amounts of money to reach the goal of the 'target amount.' The business firm or the respective individual who is looking to raise money for his project can pitch into crowdfunding websites by mentioning his 'goal amount.' Connecting to social media networks to raise funds is also a good option. Crowdfunding websites act as a bridge between the entrepreneurs (the ones who are looking for investors to start a business) and 'possible investors' (the people who are ready to contribute towards the goal using crowdfunding concepts).

For example, if an individual is trying to raise money to bear medical expenses of a deadly disease for someone who is in need of the same as the victim doesn't have any financial or family support, crowdfunding sites can come to the rescue where the required amount can be mentioned with a time period so that people who are interested in contributing can donate towards the same. I.e., raising $5000 for a neurological spinal surgery for an orphan.

When it comes to entrepreneurship, the crowdfunding concept can help double the investment efforts made compared to the traditional investment method where the entrepreneur should reach out to venture capitalists or beg his relatives for money or request the small-time investors, etc.

The crowdfunding concept gives the entrepreneurs the option to raise money from people who are interested in investing in their project without much hassle. There are many crowdfunding websites available on the market such as Kickstarter, Indiegogo, etc. These websites get their revenue from the percentage of the funds raised.

Unlike the traditional investors, the people who invest using crowdfunding websites get a sample product or reward for the investment made or an invitation to participate in the product launch, etc. It is true that most of the crowdfunding projects are based on bounties.

Crowdfunding Ethereum

Most of the Ethereum platforms support crowdfunding options as all you need to do is set up a goal and finalize a deadline for reaching the same. This can be automatically done using the 'smart contracts' concept. You can set the rules clear and trigger the contract that starts to work based on the 'already set rules.' In case one misses reaching the goal within the deadline, the amount can be returned to the respective investors. This way, the risk factor for the donors is also considerably low. The code works on an open-source platform, making it accessible to anyone who will want to use the same and all one needs to do is pay the 'gas fees' to utilize the service.

The crowdfunding options generally work based on bounties, so when you are planning to crowd-fund using the Ethereum platform, tokens can be used for the same. These tokens are responsible for keeping track of the entire participant's contact information, the details of who owns what, etc. This way the donor (the one who is investing in the crowdfunding project) can immediately own their rewards (bounties) once the donation is made. They have the option of storing the reward or selling or trading them based on their choice.

When you have successfully reached the goal within the stipulated time, and you have two different ideas to reward the donors, you can:

- If the crowdfunding was required for a digital project, you could allow the donors to use the token to 'participate in the project.'
- If the crowdfunding done was for a physical project (setting up an art exhibition), then you can send a painting (or whatever product you want to) to the donors who had sent the token back to you once the crowdfunding was successful.

This process is referred to as a 'crowdsale contract.'

So, whenever a donor is sending the Ether as the donation amount, you can set an exchange rate to the token which will enable the donors to receive a relative amount of tokens in exchange for the donated ether. How does this work? You can choose a deadline and the funding goal for the crowdfunding project. When the deadline is over, you can ping the 'crowdsale contract' and you will get your Ether if the financial goal was reached. Otherwise, the ethers will be sent back to the respective donors. The owners get to keep the tokens as a proof that they have tried to help, even if the project doesn't reach its goal.

The tokens can be created in https://ethereum.org/token and deployed. You can deploy the crowdsale contract and the token using MetaMask.

Benefits of Crowdfunding Ethereum

Crowdfunding Ethereum is a good option for people who want to invest their Ether in a good cause and also enjoy tax benefits. When the investor donates one or two ethers for particular crowdfunding projects, he or she will receive a token exchanged for the donated ether. If the project had successfully reached its goal, he or she gets to keep the token and use the same to gain entry to the entrepreneur's project. In case the crowdfunding didn't reach its goal within the specific time period, the investor gets back the Ether he donated and also gets to keep the token irrespective of the project status (which is negative).

The benefits of crowdfunding for Ethereum are:

- Refunds are possible when project goals are not met
- Crowdfunding transactions are more secure due to the smart contracts technology
- Customized contracts can be made which can benefit the investor and the recipient creating a win-win situation for both the parties.
- Since the contracts can be automatically reinforced, there is no need to worry

about an authoritative body to oversee the transactions.

General steps on how to perform crowdfunding

The decentralized way of creating a crowdfunding option with a bounty is by creating the 'token.' The tokens will keep track of the rewards, and anyone in the network who contributes by donating will get a token. This token can be traded, sold or held depending on the donor's wish. When the project successfully reaches the goal, and it is time for the donor to receive their physical reward (in case the entrepreneur has such plans), the donor will just need to exchange the token for their bounty. If the goal is not achieved, the donor gets back his donated Ether and also gets to keep the token as a reminder.

To ensure the money is spent for the purpose it was donated for, the concept of crowd equity or crowdsale is created such that any money coming out of the system needs to be approved.

- Create a fixed supply token by following the steps in the site: https://ethereum.org/token#the-code
- Deploy this and save the address.
- Create a shareholder association for 'approving the money that goes out' by following the steps in the site: https://ethereum.org/dao#the-shareholder-association
- The 'shares address' that is to be mentioned here will be the address of the token that has already been created.
- Copy the crowdsale code from the site https://ethereum.org/crowdsale to create the contract
- Enter the following details in the 'constructor parameters' section:
    - Enter the address in the 'If successful send to – address' field.
    - Enter the ethers you want to collect in the 'Funding goal in ethers' field. E.g.: 250 ethers

- o Mention the number of days (in minutes) in the 'Duration in minutes' field. E.g. 45,000 for 31 days
- o Based on the number of tokens you are putting up for sale, mention the calculated figure in the 'Ether cost of each token' field. E.g. Five ethers
- o Enter the token address you created in the 'Address of token used as reward' field.
- Mention the gas price, deploy and wait for the crowdsale to be created.
- Deposit the rewards once the page is created so that you can pay the rewards. This can be done by clicking the address of the crowdsale and then entering the amount to deposit. E.g. 50 gadgets

CHAPTER SUMMARY:

This chapter would have given you familiarization in the following:

- Crowdfunding
- Crowdfunding Ethereum and its benefits
- General steps on how to create a crowdsale contract for crowdfunding

YOUR QUICK START ACTION STEP:

To know more about the Ethereum crowdfunding concept, please visit https://ethereum.org

Chapter 7: Buying and Holding Ethereum

Chapter Seven: Buying and Holding Ethereum

'Buy and Hold' is the trusted less-risky investment strategy followed by most investors and traders irrespective of the investment being cryptocurrency investment or traditional stock market investment. The investors can reap good benefits for the patience they have shown in 'waiting for the market value to come up' by holding their 'product' (cryptocurrency or traditional shares) for a specific period. The waiting period when it comes to traditional stock marketing is minimum three years to a maximum of five to seven years.

The risk involved in this strategy is significantly low when compared to the other investing or trading methods. The trading fee is much less as there is no need to trade on a daily basis in this case. 'Buy and Hold' strategy helps the investor to save 'good tax returns' on their capital gains, as it is a long-term investment. Short-term capital gains are taxed at higher rates when compared to long-term capital gains.

'Buy and Hold' Investment Strategy – the concept

The investor buys the stocks and holds them for a long period without getting worried about the decrease in price value and the fluctuations in the market as he is looking for long-term capital gains. This process of buying and holding a stock is referred to as 'Buy and Hold' strategy. The major factor in this strategy is the vigilant attempts made to choose the right stock options to invest in by analyzing the following:

- Origin of the stock/share
- Position it holds in the stock market
- Trading history of the selected stock or share
- Number of years worth waiting
- Frequent price fluctuations (historical data table)

Once the stock is purchased, the investor will need to hold on to the stock for the decided period without allowing any external factor (market disturbances, technical issues, price fluctuations, etc.) to bother him.

Example: Jack has allocated a capital investment amount of $100,000 to start his investment portfolio. He had finalized on this amount based on his current financial status, the risk tolerance he has, current and expected tax liabilities, profit-making idea and the approximate returns he expects. He decides to invest $50,000 in stocks, $30,000 in properties and keeps the remaining $20,000 as cash. When it comes to the stocks he had purchased, he makes his mind up that he won't be doing anything with them, but will just be holding on to the stocks for five years.

Inference: Jack had invested 50% of his capital in stocks, 30% in property and the remaining 20% he had left in as cash for backup or other emergencies. He had chosen the 'buy and hold' strategy for 50% of his capital investment as he is looking at long-term capital gains. The advantage Jack gets to hold here is as time goes by, based on the stock exchange market, there is a possibility of his share weightage growing from 50% to more, which will benefit him with excellent returns.

Any investor who uses the 'buy and hold' strategy doesn't really bother about the market cycles, trade charts, price fluctuations, inflation, etc. His ultimate goal will be long-term capital gains.

'Buy and hold' Ether

The drastic change that keeps taking place in the cryptocurrency market when it comes to price value fluctuations, market scenarios, trade values, etc. makes it a risky business. To make money from this risky business, one needs to be smart. The easiest and best way to look at long-term gains is by buying and holding the crypto-token 'Ether.' The market cap and the price value of this second most popular cryptocurrency make it a worthy candidate for the same.

The strategy follows a similar set of rules and guidelines to that of traditional investing option. Instead of the stocks or shares or bonds that are bought, in this case, the crypto investor buys the coin 'Ether' and holds on to it for a specific period. The holding period is considerably low when compared to that of the stock market as the cryptocurrency market moves considerably faster. The coins can be held for a year or so, sometimes even lesser.

The Ethereum investor will need to buy the coin from a trusted Ethereum exchange, transfer the coin to an Ethereum wallet (preferably offline wallets) and hold on to the coin for a period of 6 months to 2 years. During this holding period, the investor need not worry about the market fluctuations and other external factors. After the holding period, the investor can either cash out on the coin or trade the coin for a different cryptocurrency.

Is buying and holding Ether a potential strategy?

When you have an in-depth understanding of the crypto coin and its relevant technology, it is quite an easy task for you to finalize on the strategy that will best suit you to make money. Every investor – be it beginner or an experienced cryptocurrency investor, the first thing he should keep in mind is – *If you can't afford to lose the invested amount, then it is better not to go with the decided amount.* It is always wise to start small when it comes to cryptocurrencies i.e. altcoins.

Storing the purchased Ether is the next important thing when it comes to 'Buy and Hold' strategy – it is essential to keep the coin safe during the 'holding period'. Using a hardware wallet or paper wallet would be the right choice to safeguard your coin.

Don't invest the entire money you have allocated for your investment portfolio, take it in small amounts and if the market is supportive, purchase the coins at regular intervals and keep holding on to the coins.

Buying and holding Ether will turn out to be a potential strategy due to the following reasons:

- Ether is quite stable when compared to other cryptocurrencies due to its value store
- Ether holds the second position in the cryptocurrency market when it comes to market cap value
- The Ethereum network does much more than to just hold the coins – it allows users to create a new coin (token), prepare contracts suitable to user's requirements, used to develop new dApps (decentralized application)
- The supply is limited similar to Bitcoins

Steps to buy and hold Ether

You can buy the crypto token 'Ether' from any trusted or reliable cryptocurrency exchanges. We shall use 'Poloniex' as an example:

- Sign up for a new account in the exchange 'Poloniex' by logging on to the site: https://poloniex.com/signup
- Enter the details asked for and click the 'Register' button
- Activate your account by confirming the activation link sent to your registered email address
- Once your account is activated, another mail will be sent with a confirmation letter (Don't forget to check your spam mail)
- Click on the link sent to complete your registration process
- Log in using the email ID and the created password
- Enter all the details needed to verify your profile (scanned copy of photo ID and verification photo will be expected)
- After filling the entire information, click 'Save Profile.'
- It will take three days to a week for the account to be verified after which you can use the exchange

- Once the exchange account is ready for use, you can purchase the coins using your preferred mode of payment
- The purchased Ether can then be moved to a hardware wallet or suitable offline wallet to store in a secure manner
- After the holding period, you can use the same exchange to trade your Ether for fiat money.

CHAPTER SUMMARY:

The chapter will give you a brief outline of the following:

- Buy and hold strategy in traditional investment
- Buying and holding Ether
- Benefits of the 'Buy and Hold' strategy with Ether
- Ways to try out the strategy

YOUR QUICK START ACTION STEP:

Now that you have theoretically understood the details of the 'buy and hold' strategy, you can get into action by purchasing your first ether. Try following the steps mentioned in the previous section to get started and do refer to the official website of the exchange for any clarity.

Chapter 8: How to Have Safe Ethereum Exchanges

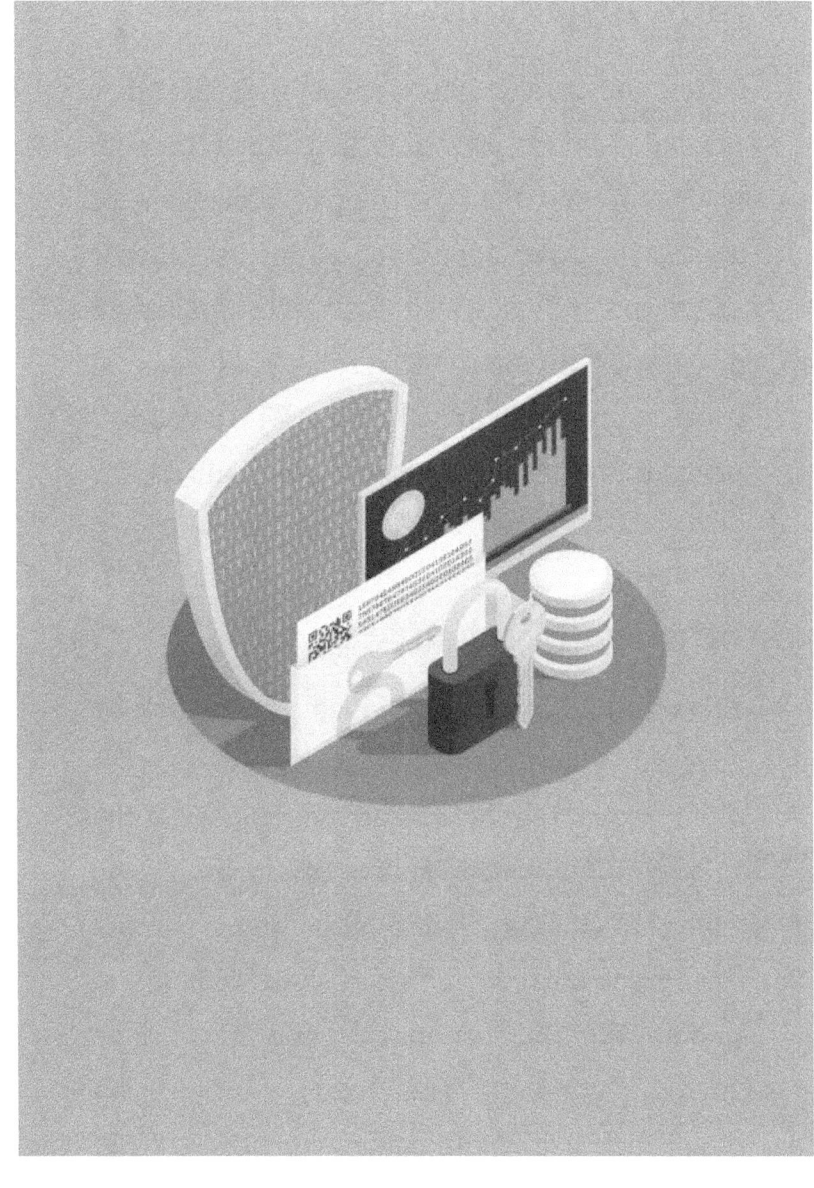

Chapter Eight: How to Have Safe Ethereum Exchanges

When you look at the current cryptocurrency market scenario, it can be said that Ethereum is one of the most growing cryptocurrencies among the other popular crypto coins. Ether is the crypto token which fuels the application and dApps used in the Ethereum platform, and if you want to buy or sell Ether (ETH), you will need an Ethereum Exchange for the same.

Ethereum Exchange

Ethereum Exchange, which is generally referred to as Cryptocurrency exchange, is an online space that acts as a bridge between the Ethereum buyers and sellers to buy or sell the Ether (ETH). This online marketplace permits the cryptocurrency buyers and sellers to initiate the transactions by offering various 'modes of payment'. The investor or trader can buy Ether using fiat currencies (USD, GBP, INR, etc.) or trade Ether with another cryptocurrency (Bitcoin, Litecoin, Bytecoin, etc.).

When you look at the traditional stock market exchange, the stock market traders purchase new stocks or sell their old stocks by checking the stock table for the price values and trade history. Similarly, cryptocurrency traders can buy or sell their Ether by checking the order table in the respective Ethereum exchange before finalizing their crypto transactions.

Trading one's Ether with the 'best-offered price' using 'market order' options or trading the coin for a lower price than the 'current ask' while buying using the 'limit order' option is possible.

Are you choosing the right Ethereum Exchange?

With more investors rushing into the cryptocurrency market in the hope of making 'quick and big money' it is crucial for these investors to choose the right cryptocurrency exchange to initiate their transactions. When an investor has decided to invest in Ether (ETH) after doing his research and devising the strategy suitable for him, he will have to get into action by selecting the right Ethereum Exchange to purchase his crypto token. There have been cases of online exchanges crashing down, securities getting compromised, falling prey to cyber-attacks and thefts, etc.; so it is vital to be cautious in choosing the right exchange.

If you would want to choose the right Ethereum exchange, the following needs to be verified and confirmed:

- The Ethereum Exchange's website needs to be secured from external threats, and all the necessary steps have to be taken for the same
- There should be high liquidity flow and easier transaction process
- The transaction fee structured should be transparent, and the exchange should be

able to provide the transaction volume, price value, liquidity risk rate, etc.
- The exchange should support various currency pairs (at least the commonly used ones – XBT/ETH, USD/XBT, ETH/GBP, etc.)
- There should be multiple payment options (PayPal, card, wire transfer, etc.)) For the investor or trader to deposit their fiat currencies for buying or trading their coins
- It is important to read the reviews and ratings to double-check the authenticity and reliability of the exchange
- The most important thing is – the exchange should be able to provide user-friendly navigation options, simple steps to proceed with the registration and transaction process.
- Too much complication can be cumbersome for the investors or traders

Avoid these mistakes while you invest in Ether

The cryptocurrency market will be giving good returns to the people who use the coins in the right way. Following FOMO (fear of missing out) and getting too greedy will burn you out brutally. Not repeating the same old mistake would be a wise choice. Let us try to avoid the following mistakes when it comes to investing in Ether:

Taking too many hasty decisions

Most beginners keep making the mistake of rushing when the markets are rolling and then getting anxious during the predictable correction. To understand this better, we will look at the example of Ethereum's spike that happened during May-June 2017. The value of Ether shot up from $90 to $400, and people started rushing in to be a part of it.

As expected, Ether corrected back to around $150, and all the new people who had rushed in and bought the coin started to panic. 50% of the new investors sold their Ether and disappeared from the market in a jiffy. If only these investors had studied about Ether before they rushed to invest or at least held on to the coin patiently for some time, they wouldn't have suffered the loss.

Rushing without understanding

As mentioned earlier, the sudden rush of people to buy Ether when the value soared high was due to greed – greed to make quick and big money. They wouldn't have lost too much if they had done their technical analysis or at least the fundamental study of what Ether is all about.

It is important to have an in-depth understanding of blockchain technology – the core of all the cryptocurrencies, before investing your hard-earned money in this digital market. When it comes to Ether, it is much more than a digital coin, the Ethereum platform offers many applications using the blockchain technology and 'smart contracts' is an important one among the lot.

No Day Trading

Day trading is a bad idea when it comes to the cryptocurrency market – be it novice trader or a seasoned professional. This market trades round the clock and is extremely volatile – though it can give millions in a second, it can also make your money into 'nothing' within seconds. Hold for long-term investments and save yourself from 'panic attacks'.

Putting all the apples in one basket

Borrowing money, investing your lifetime savings, mortgaging your house to invest in Ether is a grave mistake. Don't ever do that! Putting your entire money into the coin is dangerous. Stick to the rule – *If you can't afford to lose the invested amount, please don't.*

Making no effort to store Ether

If you don't take steps to store your Ether (ETH) safe locally or in a cold storage, you are bound to lose your coin sooner or later. However much effort these exchanges take to keep their platforms secure, you will never know when a cyber attacker will be successful in hacking the platform. It is always advisable to store your coins in a wallet that is accessible only to you.

Importance to have safe Ethereum exchanges

Unlike fiat currency, it is entirely impossible to reverse any cryptocurrency transactions which makes it all the more important to choose the right Ethereum exchanges. Entering an incorrect Ethereum wallet address and proceeding with the transaction will leave you distressed as there is no way to get the ETH back. Once gone, it is gone forever!

If you initiate your Ether transactions in an Ethereum exchange that doesn't give you the option of transferring your Ethers to a local wallet, then you are caught in the wrong place! There is no assurance that your Ethers are safe in the online wallet in the Ethereum exchange, as you never know when the platform might get hacked or the exchange goes crashing down (not that it will happen but it might!). You will not find a way to recover your Ether, as it is gone!

If you ended up with an Ethereum exchange which charges a higher transaction fee than the actual profit you might actually make, you are again at a loss! Don't be in a hurry to choose your Ethereum exchange. Do the research, look for reviews, and check for transparency of the company, etc. before you proceed with an Exchange.

Safe and reliable Ethereum Exchanges

It is essential to follow the points mentioned in the last two sections before you finalize on the Ethereum exchanges. Avoid repeating the same mistakes and revisit your Ethereum strategy plan to understand what your expectations are with respect to the investment you are going to make with the crypto coin – Ether.

The below-mentioned Ethereum Exchanges are

known to be reliable and popularly used by most of the cryptocurrency investors and traders in the crypto market:

- Coinbase
- Poloniex
- GDAX
- Bitfinex
- Kraken
- Bittrex
- CEX.IO
- CHBTC
- Bter
- YoBit

The first thing to do while choosing the right Ethereum Exchange is - to check if it supports your country and the currency you choose!

CHAPTER SUMMARY:

This chapter will have taken you through the concepts of Cryptocurrency Exchanges along with the following:

- Ethereum Exchanges

- Mistakes to be avoided while investing in Ether
- Steps to take while choosing the right exchange
- Importance to have a safe Ethereum Exchange
- Popular Ethereum Exchanges

YOUR QUICK START ACTION STEP:

After going through this chapter, you would by now have understood the importance of choosing the right exchange for a safe tension-free transaction. To know more, please visit https://www.coinworld.io/Bitcoin-ethereum-exchanges/.

Bonus Chapter: Risk Management Strategies with Ethereum Investing

BONUS Chapter: Risk Management Strategies with Ethereum Investing

It is essential to take all the required steps to manage the risk associated with cryptocurrency, especially Ether (ETH) as the extreme fluctuation and volatility in the crypto market can result in huge financial loss if not taken care of during the early stages. With more people and business enterprises showing interest in Ethereum because of the additional feature it provides with the blockchain technology, it is time to take control of the potential risks and work on a strategy to overcome or manage the same.

Following articles, blogs and discussions with respect to Ethereum will help you to keep track of the market happenings and give an option to evaluate the risk at a much earlier stage. When you come across discussions backed up with sensible reasoning, it is always a good idea to assess the situation and take the necessary steps to avoid unexpected losses. Most of the chat rooms discuss possible price dips, trading charts, etc., but as a smart investor or trader, it is crucial to differentiate between the discussions which talk 'sense' from the ones which talk 'nonsense.'

Get the facts right before you make your decision as most of the time when popular crypto coins such as Bitcoin and Ether go low they come back to a stable price value soon, so be patient and don't take decisions in fear.

Taking a proper decision by following a discipline in the trading or investing pattern to manage the risk will help you strategize on the right 'risk management plan' when it comes to Ethereum.

Taking the right decision for effective 'Risk Management.'

The financial market saw a considerable change in 2017 when the two coins – Bitcoin and Ether rolled everything topsy-turvy. The crypto market which trades around 1200 crypto coins saw an increase from $17.7 billion in the beginning of 2017 to $236 billion as on date in its aggregate market capitalization. This is roughly around 1000% in a year. Ethereum had a rise in price value by close to 3700%, and this spiky increase is due to the potential blockchain technology. More than 150 organizations (including nine famous names) are testing various projects on Ethereum blockchain in the energy sector, financial sector, etc. through the Enterprise Ethereum Alliance.

For an effective risk management strategy for Ethereum, it is vital to keep yourself updated on the market trends instead of completely concentrating on the capital gains. If you would like to have a strong Ethereum Investment portfolio, it is essential to check on the following:

- Make sure to have in-depth knowledge of Ethereum blockchain, different ways to use smart contracts, benefits of

creating new crypto tokens and the market history of Ether.
- Try to analyze the reasons behind frequent price fluctuations by going through the trading history on quarterly basis. It will help you identify the patterns of the decrease and can also show you the possible reasons behind the same (Though the crypto market is volatile, it is better to do the homework!)
- Patience is important. Making decisions when you are emotionally disturbed by the market fluctuation will result in a complete fiasco. Be confident and make decisions based on the facts.

Importance and benefits of Risk Management Strategies

Calculated analysis and cautious assessments made by an Ethereum investor will help him devise a proper risk management plan. Rumors and unnecessary media hype on Ethereum's price value decreases will not affect an investor who is already equipped with his risk management strategy just in case he gets caught in an unforeseen situation.

Having a proper plan in place will reduce the risk of losing out on capital investment or suffering heavy losses and save the investor from falling prey to 'media hypes', 'social media rumors', etc. It is important to concentrate on the 'idea that led to the currency' rather than focusing on the currency alone, i.e., as an Ethereum investor you should know that this platform offers smart contracts technology, allows to create new tokens, etc. and it is clearly much more than just a coin 'Ether.' Focus on the idea and technology!

When you are in a position to appreciate and implement the right risk management strategy, then as an investor you get benefitted in the following ways:

- Maintaining a steady Ethereum investment portfolio
- Potential chances to reduce risks

- Having a clear focus on the financial objectives
- Enjoy more returns and fewer losses
- Ability to study and recognize the market better
- Able to predict a change much before it happens
- Foreseeing major possibilities of benefits and risks based on the historical data (trade history, market charts, etc.)

Ways to implement

It is important to understand the market cap of Ether to check the weightage of the currency in a particular period. To implement an effective risk management strategy, it is necessary to:

- Comprehend the investment allocation
- Keep track of the market cap table
- Assess the risk tolerance level
- Finalize on the Ethereum strategy which would help in making money as per your financial goals

- Review the risk management plan on a fortnight basis to 'balance your financial scenario.'

CHAPTER SUMMARY:

This chapter deals with risk management strategy and gets into details of the following:

- Risk Management Strategy in Ethereum
- Taking the right decision for effective risk management
- Risk Management Strategy and its benefits
- Ways to implement the strategy

YOUR QUICK START ACTION STEP:

Once you have chosen your mode of investment with Ethereum, work on devising a strategic plan to handle the possible risk that you might face during the process. You can check the previous section and follow the points mentioned to create an effective risk management strategy

Conclusion

Thank you once again for owning this book!

I hope this book was able to help you understand the various Ethereum strategies that can be implemented to earn that extra buck you always wanted to earn.

The next step is to work out a strategic plan for your relevant portfolio, decide on the best strategy which will help in achieving your financial goals and go ahead confidently to implement the chosen Ethereum strategy. This book's primary objective is to take you through the various Ethereum strategies, the ways to implement them and the steps to manage risks that might occur due to unforeseen circumstances.

Finally, if this book has helped you in any way, then I'd like to ask you for a favor. Would you please be kind enough to leave a review for this book on Amazon? It'd be greatly appreciated!

Thank you and good luck!

About the Author

Gavin S. Finney is a Bitcoin and cryptocurrency investor who have written several books on the subject.

As a successful investor, he then got interested in digital currency and Bitcoin during its early stages, but got frustrated learning the technical topic.

Gavin wanted a method that he could easily learn from in order to understand all about digital currency and how to make money out of it. He soon discovered a teaching series online that made him learn faster and better.

Applying the same approach, Gavin successfully made his first digital currency transaction which triggered the start of his digital currency success.

With the books that he writes on the subject matter, he aims to provide readers with great value and in the hopes that they too can experience the same success investing and making money from cryptocurrency.

www.ingramcontent.com/pod-product-compliance
Lightning Source LLC
Chambersburg PA
CBHW070143230526
45471CB00002B/488